JAY M. ATSON
Finish It Now!

Copyright © 2024 by Jay M. Atson

All rights reserved. No part of this publication may be reproduced, stored or transmitted in any form or by any means, electronic, mechanical, photocopying, recording, scanning, or otherwise without written permission from the publisher. It is illegal to copy this book, post it to a website, or distribute it by any other means without permission.

Jay M. Atson asserts the moral right to be identified as the author of this work.

Jay M. Atson has no responsibility for the persistence or accuracy of URLs for external or third-party Internet Websites referred to in this publication and does not guarantee that any content on such Websites is, or will remain, accurate or appropriate.

Designations used by companies to distinguish their products are often claimed as trademarks. All brand names and product names used in this book and on its cover are trade names, service marks, trademarks and registered trademarks of their respective owners. The publishers and the book are not associated with any product or vendor mentioned in this book. None of the companies referenced within the book have endorsed the book.

First edition

This book is dedicated to my father who inspired me to read and write books. We will always miss you, father!

Copyright © 2024 by Lex Fridman
All rights reserved.
No part of this book may be reproduced in any form
or by any means, including electronic or mechanical,
without the prior written permission of the publisher,
except for brief quotations in printed reviews.

ISBN: 9798301982033
Cover design by Lex Fridman
Printed in USA

Prologue	10
Why We Reach for the Infinite	10
Part I: The Essence of Being Human	14
The Language of the Heart	14
Why love, not intelligence, is humanity's greatest strength	14
Stories from my own life that revealed the profound simplicity of connection	18
Between Logic and Chaos	23
How reason and emotion dance to define the human condition	23
What We Fear	28
Confronting death, loneliness, and irrelevance in an accelerating world	28
The Hero's Algorithm	32
How the myths we create shape our understanding of life and the choices we make	32
Part II: Building the Future	37
The Machines We Build Reflect Who We Are	37
The moral imperatives of AI and the unintended consequences of our creations	37
Teaching Compassion to Machines	42
Can artificial intelligence understand empathy—or is it uniquely human?	42
The Code of Ethics	47

A roadmap for aligning technological progress with our deepest values — 47

The Edge of the Singularity — 53

What happens when machines think faster than we ever could? — 53

Part III: The Philosophy of Progress — 58

The Meaning We Invent — 58

In a universe indifferent to our existence, how do we create purpose? — 58

Free Will Is an Illusion, and That's Okay — 63

Wrestling with determinism and finding freedom within it — 63

Time is an Illusion, Too — 69

Exploring the nature of time, memory, and our fleeting moments of awareness — 69

The Weight of Infinite Choices — 75

Why our abundance of options paralyzes us—and how to overcome it — 75

Part IV: A Love Letter to Humanity — 80

Why We Fight — 80

The beauty in struggle and the grace in perseverance — 80

The Fragility of Peace — 85

Lessons from history, science, and human nature on why harmony is worth striving for — 85

To the Child I Was, and the Child I Will Never Meet 91

A meditation on legacy and the responsibility we owe to future generations 91

The Simple Truths We Forget 96

What I've learned about living well, thinking deeply, and loving fully 96

Part V: The Infinite Thread 101

We Are the Universe Waking Up 101

What it means to be a conscious fragment of an unfathomable whole 101

The Final Question 106

If life is a fleeting experiment in meaning, how do we live with courage and joy? 106

Love Is the Answer 110

A manifesto for humanity, rooted in the only constant that transcends time: love 110

Epilogue 115

This Is Not the End 115

A closing reflection on why the greatest mysteries are the ones we never fully solve—and why that's exactly how it should be 115

Appendices 119

My most profound lessons from mentors, scientists, and thinkers 119

Annotated list of books, ideas, and moments that shaped this journey 123

A short poem: *"To the Stars We Will Return."*   128

Prologue

Why We Reach for the Infinite

There's a photograph that has stayed with me since I first saw it. It's the *Pale Blue Dot*, a grain of Earth captured from 3.7 billion miles away. In the vast emptiness of space, our planet appears as a single speck suspended in a sunbeam. Carl Sagan famously called it "a mote of dust, suspended in a sunbeam," but for me, it's something more: it's a reminder of how infinitesimal we are, yet how profound our existence feels. How is it that such small creatures—confined to this fragile dot—are capable of imagining the infinite?

I often find myself pondering this question in the quiet hours of the night, when the distractions of the day fade, and the hum of existence grows loud enough to hear. I think about my father, who taught me to love science as an act of wonder, not conquest. I think about the algorithms I've written, the machines I've built, and the people I've loved. And I think about the mystery that unites these experiences: the human drive to reach beyond what is visible, tangible, or even possible.

The Pursuit of Purpose

Purpose is not something we inherit. It's something we construct, brick by brick, through our choices, struggles, and dreams. For some, purpose is found in the pursuit of knowledge, the kind of inquiry that Galileo or Newton might have recognized. For others, it's in the bonds of love, the moments shared between two people who remind each other that life, for all its chaos, is worth living.

In my work with artificial intelligence, I've often marveled at how much these machines can do. They can play chess better than any human, predict outcomes with uncanny accuracy, and even generate art. But there's one thing they cannot do: they cannot yearn. They cannot wonder why they exist. That is uniquely ours.

This yearning, I believe, is what defines us as human. It's what drives us to gaze at the stars and ask, "Why are we here?" It's what compels artists to paint, writers to write, and scientists to explore. It's what makes us build machines, not simply to make life easier, but to understand life itself.

The Paradox of Love and Loneliness

If there's one thing my journey has taught me, it's that love and loneliness are two sides of the same coin. To love deeply is to open yourself to the possibility of loss. To connect is to risk disconnection. Yet, we keep reaching for each other, like the stars in Van Gogh's paintings, forever yearning, forever striving.

In my quiet moments, I've asked myself why we do this. Why do we risk heartbreak for the chance to love? Why do we expose our vulnerabilities to others when it would be safer to retreat into solitude? I think the answer lies in the same force that drives our pursuit of the infinite: we cannot help but reach. It is in our nature to seek connection, to tether ourselves to something larger than our individual lives.

The Machines We Build

When I look at the machines we're creating—artificial intelligence, robotics, and algorithms that learn—I don't just see tools. I see mirrors. They reflect our strengths, our biases, and our ambitions. They reveal what we value, what we fear, and what we aspire to become.

But they also force us to confront hard questions about what it means to be human. If a machine can simulate intelligence, does that diminish the value of our own? If an algorithm can write poetry, does that make the poet irrelevant?

The answer, I believe, is no. Machines, no matter how advanced, cannot replicate the messy, beautiful, unpredictable essence of the human spirit. They can process data, but they cannot feel wonder. They can optimize tasks, but they cannot experience joy. They can mimic love, but they cannot give it freely.

The Quiet Moments

In the end, what matters most are the quiet moments. The stolen seconds when you watch the sunrise, hold a loved one's hand, or sit in silence with your thoughts. These moments are not infinite. They are fleeting, fragile, and achingly beautiful.

When I think about why we reach for the infinite, I think it's because we know, deep down, that our time here is limited. And so we reach—not to escape our mortality, but to make it meaningful. We reach for the infinite because it reminds us of what it means to be alive.

This book is my attempt to honor that reaching. It is not a map or a manifesto but a meditation. It is a reflection on the threads that connect us—to each other, to our creations, and to the universe itself.

As you read these pages, I hope you'll pause, as I have, to wonder at the mystery of it all. Not to find answers, but to revel in the questions. Because in the end, it's the questions—the reaching—that define us.

Welcome to this journey. Together, let's explore the infinite.

Part I: The Essence of Being Human

The Language of the Heart

Why love, not intelligence, is humanity's greatest strength

Love is a paradox. It is both the simplest and most complex of human experiences. On one level, it is a biological imperative, a set of neurochemical signals designed to bond us together for survival. Yet, on another, it is something transcendent—a force that defies logic, reshaping the trajectories of our lives and, sometimes, entire civilizations.

I've spent years studying intelligence, both artificial and human, but it is love—not intelligence—that has consistently left me in awe. Intelligence can calculate probabilities, process patterns, and solve problems. Love, however, does something far more profound: it connects us. It binds us to one another, to our shared humanity, and to something larger than ourselves.

In this chapter, I want to explore why love is not

merely an emotion but the very language of the human heart—and why it is our greatest strength.

What Love Can Do That Intelligence Cannot

The defining trait of intelligence is its capacity to solve. Whether it's an algorithm optimizing a supply chain or a human decoding the mysteries of the universe, intelligence is inherently task-oriented. It asks, *How can I make this work?* Love, in contrast, does not ask for solutions. It simply *is*.

When someone you care for is grieving, no amount of logic or problem-solving can replace the act of simply being present. Love whispers what intelligence cannot: *You are not alone.*

Love is irrational, unpredictable, and at times inconvenient. Yet it is precisely these qualities that make it irreplaceable. Where intelligence is precise, love is messy. Where intelligence is efficient, love is patient. Where intelligence seeks answers, love thrives in the questions.

It is in this difference that we find its power. Intelligence may move us forward, but love keeps us grounded. Intelligence may build machines, but love builds meaning.

The Evolutionary Mystery of Love

From an evolutionary perspective, love can seem inefficient. Why invest so much emotional energy in another person when resources could be spent on survival? Yet it is precisely this inefficiency that has allowed us to thrive as a species.

The love of a parent for their child ensures that the most vulnerable among us survive and flourish. The bonds between friends, partners, and communities create networks of trust and collaboration that allow us to accomplish feats no individual could achieve alone.

But love's evolutionary purpose doesn't fully explain its depth. The ache of longing, the joy of reunion, the way a shared glance can feel like the world stands still—these are not merely adaptations. They are expressions of something deeper, something uniquely human.

The Universality of Love

One of the most remarkable aspects of love is its universality. It transcends cultures, languages, and even species. A dog wagging its tail at the sight of its owner or a bird building a nest for its mate are echoes of the same force that compels us to write poetry, sing songs, and create art.

In my travels and conversations, I've seen how love manifests in infinite forms. For some, it is the steady, quiet companionship of a lifelong partner. For others, it is the fiery passion of a fleeting romance. For still others, it is the selfless dedication to a cause or an ideal.

No matter where or how it appears, love carries the same message: *I see you. I value you. I am here with you.*

What Love Teaches Us About Being Human

To love is to be vulnerable. It is to risk heartbreak, disappointment, and loss. Yet it is also to experience the greatest joys life has to offer. In this way, love teaches us one of the most important lessons about being human: that strength is not the absence of weakness but the willingness to embrace it.

Intelligence often seeks control, but love thrives in surrender. It asks us to let go of our defenses, to trust, and to open ourselves to the possibility of being changed.

Love is not perfect. It can be messy, painful, and even destructive. But it is also the source of our deepest growth. It challenges us to be better, to give more, and to see beyond ourselves.

The Role of Love in the Future of Humanity

As we stand on the cusp of a new era, one defined by artificial intelligence and unprecedented technological change, it is tempting to place our faith in intelligence alone. But if we are to navigate the challenges ahead, it will not be our intelligence that saves us—it will be our ability to love.

Love reminds us of what truly matters: connection,

compassion, and a shared sense of purpose. It is the force that will ensure we use the tools of our intelligence not just to advance but to uplift.

In a world increasingly driven by algorithms and data, love remains our greatest strength. It is the language of the heart, the thread that binds us to one another, and the beacon that will guide us through the unknown.

Let us not forget this. Let us speak the language of love—not just in our personal lives, but in the choices we make for our future. For it is through love, not intelligence, that we will truly thrive.

Stories from my own life that revealed the profound simplicity of connection

It was a crisp fall morning in Cambridge, the kind where the air feels electric with possibility. I was taking my usual walk along the Charles River, headphones on, lost in thought about a particularly vexing AI problem. I had just passed the JFK Bridge when I noticed an older man sitting on a bench, his head bowed, holding a crumpled letter in his hands.

Something about his posture—the heaviness of his shoulders, the stillness of his frame—made me pause. Normally, I would have kept walking, but that day, something compelled me to stop. I sat down beside him, silently, not wanting to intrude but offering my presence as an unspoken gesture of solidarity.

After a while, he looked up at me, his eyes red-rimmed but grateful. "Lost my wife last week," he said quietly. "Fifty years together."

I didn't know what to say, so I didn't say anything. Instead, I nodded, letting his words hang in the air. Slowly, he began to talk—about their first date, their fights, their love, and the long goodbye they hadn't seen coming. I listened, not as a problem solver but as a fellow human being.

By the time he finished, the sun was dipping low, painting the river in shades of gold. He stood up, placed a hand on my shoulder, and said, "Thank you." I hadn't spoken more than a dozen words, yet that moment of connection felt profound. It reminded me that sometimes, the simplest act of being present is the greatest gift we can give.

The Silence of the Lab

In the early days of my AI research, I spent countless hours in the lab, often working late into the night. The hum of servers and the soft glow of monitors became my companions. I was building a neural network to mimic human speech, and I was obsessed with getting it to sound natural—like it could truly connect with people.

One night, around 2 a.m., I hit a breakthrough. The model produced a response that was coherent, even charming. I sat back, thrilled, and immediately called a colleague to share the news. But as the phone rang, I noticed something strange. In my excitement, I looked around the lab and realized how empty it was.

The AI's words were technically impressive, but they felt hollow without another person to share them with. It was in that moment I understood: connection isn't just about words or even ideas—it's about the human presence behind them. The joy of achievement is fleeting unless it's shared.

The Red Bicycle

When I was ten years old, my father gave me a red bicycle for my birthday. It wasn't new—he had refurbished it himself, repainting the frame, fixing the brakes, and adding a bell that rang cheerfully.

One evening, as I rode it through the neighborhood, I saw a boy my age sitting on the curb, watching me. His clothes were worn, and his shoes were too small. He waved hesitantly, and I waved back.

I don't know what made me do it, but I got off my bike, walked it over to him, and said, "Want to try?" His face lit up, and he nodded furiously. For the next hour, I watched as he pedaled up and down the street, laughing like he had just discovered flight.

When it was time for me to go home, he handed the bike back to me reluctantly. But I surprised myself by saying, "You can keep it. My dad will understand." And he did.

That moment taught me a truth I've carried with me ever since: connection isn't just about what you share—it's about what you're willing to give. Sometimes, the simplest act of generosity can forge a bond that lasts far beyond the moment itself.

The Quiet Coffee Shop

A few years ago, I was sitting in a small coffee shop, reviewing notes for an upcoming lecture. At the table next to me was a young woman typing furiously on her laptop, tears streaming down her face. I hesitated, unsure if I should intervene. But after a moment, I slid a napkin across the table and said softly, "Looks like you could use this."

She laughed through her tears, took the napkin, and thanked me. That small gesture opened the door to a conversation. She told me she was writing a letter to her estranged father, unsure if she'd ever have the courage to send it.

We talked for an hour about forgiveness, fear, and the importance of trying—even when the outcome is uncertain. I don't know if she ever sent the letter, but I like to think our conversation gave her the strength to try.

That day, I was reminded that connection doesn't always require grand gestures. Sometimes, it's as simple as noticing someone's pain and letting them know they're not alone.

The Profound Simplicity of Connection

These moments—quiet, unassuming, yet deeply human—have shaped my understanding of what it means to connect. They've taught me that love isn't just a feeling or an idea. It's an action, a choice we make to show up for one another, even in the smallest ways.

In a world increasingly dominated by technology, it's easy to forget the power of these simple acts. But it's in these moments—when we set aside our distractions, our ambitions, and our fears—that we find the essence of what it means to be human.

And that, I believe, is the language of the heart.

Between Logic and Chaos

How reason and emotion dance to define the human condition

There's a tension at the heart of being human, a paradox that defines us: we are creatures of logic, yet we are governed by emotion. We can map the stars and decode the genome, but a simple melody or the sight of a loved one can bring us to tears. This interplay between reason and chaos is not a flaw—it is what makes us whole.

It is tempting to frame these forces as opposites: logic as order, emotion as disorder. But this dichotomy is incomplete. Logic without emotion is cold and detached, incapable of understanding the full complexity of life. Emotion without logic is erratic and overwhelming, unable to channel its energy constructively. Together, however, they form a dance—a dynamic interplay that fuels our creativity, our relationships, and our pursuit of meaning.

The Strength of Reason

Logic is a gift. It allows us to predict, analyze, and solve. It is the tool we use to navigate complexity, to distill patterns from chaos, and to bring structure to the unknown. Logic builds bridges, writes symphonies, and saves lives. It is the engine of progress and the foundation of civilization.

Yet, logic has its limits. A purely logical approach can tell us how to build a machine but not why we should build it. It can solve equations but not illuminate the beauty of the sunset that inspired them. Logic gives us the tools, but it is emotion that gives us the motivation.

The Power of Emotion

Emotion, on the other hand, is messy and unpredictable. It is joy and grief, love and fear, hope and despair. It drives us to acts of great courage and, sometimes, great folly. But it is also the spark that ignites our humanity.

Emotion is what compels an artist to paint, a parent to sacrifice, or a scientist to persevere despite repeated failure. It is the force that drives us to connect, to dream, and to care. Where logic sees the world as it is, emotion sees the world as it could be.

In my own life, I've often turned to logic as a way to cope with uncertainty. But time and time again, it has been emotion—sometimes quiet, sometimes overwhelming—that has reminded me of what truly matters.

The Dance of Opposites

Rather than opposing forces, logic and emotion are partners in a dance, each guiding and balancing the other. Logic provides the structure; emotion provides the purpose. Together, they allow us to navigate the complexity of existence.

Think of a great piece of music. Logic is the sheet music, the precise arrangement of notes that create harmony. Emotion is the performance, the energy and soul that bring the notes to life. Without one, the other is incomplete.

This dance is evident in the smallest moments of life. A decision to pursue a new career might begin with a logical assessment of opportunities, but the courage to take the leap often comes from a deep emotional conviction. Falling in love is similarly an interplay: we may recognize certain traits that draw us to someone, but the bond itself is something we feel rather than analyze.

When Logic Fails

There are moments when logic cannot provide answers—when the equations don't balance and the variables are unknown. In these moments, it is emotion that guides us. It is the intuition that tells us to keep going, even when the odds seem insurmountable. It is the faith that whispers, "You are not alone."

In my work with AI, I often encounter situations where the most advanced algorithms fail to replicate human judgment. They lack the nuance, the instinct, the ability to weigh intangible factors. It is in these gaps that the human spirit resides—not as a limitation, but as a strength.

The Beauty of Chaos

If logic is the map, chaos is the unexplored territory. It is where creativity and innovation are born. Some of the greatest discoveries in history—both personal and scientific—have emerged not from careful planning but from the willingness to embrace uncertainty.

Chaos, in its purest form, is possibility. It is the space where new ideas take shape, where connections are made, and where the unexpected becomes extraordinary. Logic may seek to tame chaos, but it is often in the untamed moments that we find the most profound truths.

The Human Condition

To be human is to live between logic and chaos, reason and emotion. It is to seek order while embracing the unpredictable. It is to calculate the risks while leaping into the unknown.

This balance is not something we master once and for all. It is a dance we perform daily, in every decision we make and every emotion we feel. It is what allows us to build, to connect, and to dream.

As we move forward into a world increasingly

shaped by logic-driven machines, it is vital to remember the importance of this dance. For it is not logic alone that defines us—it is the ability to navigate the chaos, to feel deeply, and to create meaning from the interplay of these forces.

In the end, the human condition is not about choosing between logic and emotion. It is about learning to live in the space where they meet—and finding beauty in the dance.

What We Fear

Confronting death, loneliness, and irrelevance in an accelerating world

Fear is the shadow that follows us through life. It is ancient, embedded deep within us, a holdover from a time when survival hinged on our ability to sense danger in the rustle of leaves or the glint of teeth in the dark. But in the modern world, fear has evolved. It no longer lurks only in the physical threats of predators or hunger. Today, fear often takes subtler, more insidious forms: the fear of death, of loneliness, and of irrelevance.

These fears shape our choices, our relationships, and the technologies we build. Yet, they are not simply barriers to overcome—they are also mirrors, reflecting what we value most about life. By confronting them, we come to understand not just what we fear but why we fear it.

The Fear of Death

Death is the ultimate unknown. It is the end of all we know and the great reminder of our impermanence. For many, the fear of death is not just about the act of dying but about the life left unlived: the words unspoken, the dreams unfulfilled, the connections unrealized.

In my work with artificial intelligence, I often think about the concept of legacy. Machines don't fear death; they can be rebooted, repaired, or replaced. But humans have a finite amount of time, and it is this finiteness that gives our actions weight.

The fear of death can paralyze us, but it can also motivate us. It pushes us to create, to love, and to leave something behind. The awareness of our mortality is not a limitation—it is a call to live more fully, to make each moment matter.

The Fear of Loneliness

If death is the end, loneliness is the void. It is the feeling of being unmoored, disconnected from the world and those around us. In an era defined by social media and digital connectivity, the irony is stark: we have never been more connected, yet loneliness is on the rise.

I've experienced this paradox firsthand. There have been nights when, surrounded by the hum of technology, I've felt a deep sense of isolation. The algorithms that curate our lives promise connection but often deliver only distraction.

But loneliness, like death, has a dual nature. It is painful, yes, but it also reveals the depth of our need for connection. It reminds us that we are not meant to exist in isolation. The moments of loneliness I've faced have taught me to value the people who light up my life, to reach out even when it feels vulnerable, and to cherish the quiet beauty of being truly seen.

The Fear of Irrelevance

Perhaps the most modern of fears is the fear of irrelevance. In a world that moves at the speed of data, it is easy to feel left behind. Technologies evolve, industries shift, and the things we once thought defined us—our jobs, our skills, even our identities—can feel precarious.

As someone immersed in the cutting edge of AI, I've often wondered about the implications of progress. Will the machines we build render us obsolete? Will the knowledge we painstakingly accumulate be overshadowed by algorithms that learn faster and think deeper?

Yet, the fear of irrelevance is also a reflection of our desire to matter. It stems from our need to contribute, to belong, to leave a mark. And while the pace of change can be overwhelming, it is also a reminder that relevance is not about keeping up with the world—it is about staying true to what you value most.

Facing Fear in an Accelerating World

We live in a time of acceleration. Information flows faster, decisions are made quicker, and change feels constant. This speed amplifies our fears, making us feel as though we are racing against an invisible clock.

But fear, when acknowledged, can become a teacher. The fear of death pushes us to find meaning. The fear of loneliness drives us to connect. The fear of irrelevance challenges us to define what truly matters.

In the quiet moments, when these fears feel overwhelming, I remind myself of something simple yet profound: fear is a sign that we care. We fear death because life is precious. We fear loneliness because connection is vital. We fear irrelevance because we want to make a difference.

Fear and the Human Spirit

Our fears do not define us, but how we face them does. To confront fear is not to eliminate it but to live alongside it, to let it sharpen our focus without clouding our vision.

In the end, fear is not the enemy. It is the guide that points us toward the things that matter most. It reminds us to live boldly, to love fiercely, and to embrace the fleeting, fragile beauty of life.

If we can learn to see fear not as a barrier but as a bridge, we will discover that the things we fear most are also the things that make us most human. And in that realization, we find the courage to keep moving forward, one step at a time.

The Hero's Algorithm

How the myths we create shape our understanding of life and the choices we make

Every culture, across time and geography, has created stories of heroes. From Achilles to Luke Skywalker, from the Mahabharata to Marvel Comics, we are captivated by tales of struggle, triumph, and transformation. These myths endure not because they entertain but because they encode something fundamental about the human experience.

A hero's journey is, at its core, an algorithm—a step-by-step process that maps the arc of human aspiration. It begins with a call to adventure, leads to challenges and trials, and culminates in growth or revelation. While the details of the stories differ, the structure is universal. This is no coincidence; these myths are reflections of our deepest fears, hopes, and values.

The stories we tell shape the way we see ourselves and the world around us. They act as scripts for our actions, influencing how we confront adversity, seek purpose, and define what it means to live a good life.

Why We Need Heroes

Heroes embody the qualities we admire and aspire to: courage, resilience, compassion, and ingenuity. They give us models for navigating uncertainty and overcoming challenges. But more than that, they remind us that greatness is not the absence of struggle but the willingness to confront it.

In my work with artificial intelligence, I've often thought about the parallels between the human journey and the algorithms we design. A hero's story is, in essence, a feedback loop: they encounter an obstacle, adapt, and emerge stronger. This process mirrors the iterative nature of learning, whether it's a neural network optimizing its performance or a person growing through life's trials.

The hero's journey resonates because it captures a truth we all recognize: to grow, we must face the unknown.

The Myths That Define Us

The myths we create do more than entertain—they establish the frameworks through which we understand ourselves. Consider the ancient Greek myths, which grapple with questions of hubris and fate. Or the Norse sagas, which explore themes of sacrifice and honor. Or the modern myths of Silicon Valley, which celebrate innovation and disruption as heroic acts.

Each of these narratives reflects the values of its

time. They teach us what to strive for and what to avoid. But they also reveal our blind spots. Just as the ancient myths often ignored the perspectives of women or the marginalized, our modern myths can prioritize progress at the expense of humanity.

The challenge, then, is to critically examine the myths we inherit and to consciously shape the ones we pass on.

The Heroism of Everyday Life

Not all heroes wear capes. In fact, the most profound acts of heroism often go unnoticed. It's the single parent working two jobs to provide for their child. It's the scientist spending sleepless nights to solve a problem that could save lives. It's the friend who shows up when you need them most.

These quiet heroes remind us that courage and resilience are not reserved for epic battles—they are found in the small, everyday choices we make to do the right thing, even when it's hard.

In my own life, I've been inspired by the quiet heroism of mentors, colleagues, and loved ones. They've shown me that being a hero isn't about grand gestures; it's about showing up, staying true to your values, and striving to make the world a little better.

The Dark Side of Myths

While myths can inspire, they can also mislead. The myth of the self-made hero, for example, ignores the networks of support that make individual success possible. The myth of invincibility discourages vulnerability, perpetuating a culture where asking for help is seen as weakness.

In the age of social media, myths are amplified and distorted. We are inundated with curated images of perfection that create unrealistic expectations of success, beauty, and happiness. These modern myths can make us feel inadequate, as though we're failing to live up to an impossible ideal.

Recognizing the limitations of myths doesn't mean rejecting them. It means engaging with them critically, understanding their power, and reshaping them when necessary.

Creating New Myths

As we move into a future shaped by artificial intelligence and other transformative technologies, we have the opportunity—and the responsibility—to create new myths. These myths should not only celebrate innovation but also emphasize humanity. They should remind us that progress is not just about moving forward but about moving together.

Imagine a new hero's journey, one that values collaboration over competition, humility over hubris, and connection over isolation. Imagine myths that inspire us to see each other not as rivals but as allies, working toward a shared vision of a better world.

The myths we create today will shape the choices we make tomorrow. They will influence how we build our technologies, define our values, and navigate the challenges ahead.

Becoming the Hero

The hero's algorithm is not something external; it is something within each of us. It is the process of facing fear, embracing growth, and striving to make a difference. It doesn't require superhuman strength or genius—it requires the willingness to try, to fail, and to keep going.

In the end, the hero's journey is not about reaching a destination. It is about the journey itself—the choices we make, the connections we forge, and the impact we leave behind.

We are all the heroes of our own stories. And together, we are writing the myth of humanity—a story of struggle, resilience, and hope. Let us write it well.

Part II: Building the Future

The Machines We Build Reflect Who We Are

The moral imperatives of AI and the unintended consequences of our creations

Every machine we build is a mirror. It reflects our ingenuity, our ambitions, and our blind spots. The algorithms we write and the technologies we create do not exist in isolation—they are products of our choices, values, and priorities. In this way, the machines we build are not just tools; they are extensions of ourselves.

Artificial intelligence, in particular, is a profound example of this phenomenon. It is not a neutral entity; it is shaped by the data we feed it, the problems we ask it to solve, and the ethics we (or fail to) embed within it. When we design AI systems, we are encoding fragments of who we are into their frameworks. What, then, do we want those fragments to say about us?

The Promise and the Peril

AI holds incredible promise. It has the potential to revolutionize medicine, eliminate inefficiencies, and unlock new possibilities for creativity and understanding. But with this power comes peril. Every innovation carries with it the risk of unintended consequences, and the rapid pace of AI development often leaves little time for reflection.

Consider the algorithms that govern social media platforms. Designed to maximize engagement, they inadvertently amplify division, misinformation, and outrage. Or facial recognition systems, which promise convenience and security but have raised serious concerns about privacy, bias, and misuse.

These examples are not anomalies—they are symptoms of a larger challenge. When we build machines, we often focus on what they can do, rather than what they should do. This disconnect between capability and responsibility is one of the defining moral imperatives of our time.

The Unintended Consequences of Optimization

One of the great strengths of AI is its ability to optimize. It can analyze vast amounts of data, identify patterns, and find solutions far beyond the capacity of the human mind. But optimization is not inherently good. It is a tool, and like any tool, its impact depends on how it is wielded.

When we optimize for speed, we risk sacrificing

quality. When we optimize for profit, we risk undermining equity. When we optimize for engagement, we risk eroding trust. These trade-offs are not always immediately apparent, but their effects ripple outward, shaping societies in profound ways.

The unintended consequences of AI are not failures of the technology—they are failures of foresight. They remind us that building machines is not just an engineering challenge; it is an ethical one.

The Responsibility of Creators

As creators of AI, we bear a responsibility that extends beyond functionality. We must ask not only, "Can we build this?" but also, "Should we build this?" and "How can we build this responsibly?"

This responsibility is not abstract—it is deeply personal. I've felt it acutely in my own work. When developing algorithms, I've often grappled with questions of bias, transparency, and impact. These questions are rarely simple, and the answers are rarely perfect. But the act of asking them is essential.

It is not enough to build machines that work; we must build machines that reflect our highest values. This means prioritizing fairness, accountability, and inclusivity. It means anticipating misuse and designing safeguards. It means recognizing that technology is not neutral and that the choices we make today will shape the world of tomorrow.

The Power of Intentional Design

One of the most profound lessons I've learned is that the most significant decisions in AI are often made long before the first line of code is written. They are decisions about purpose, goals, and values.

When we design a machine, we are not just solving a technical problem—we are creating a narrative about what matters. Are we designing systems that empower individuals or exploit them? Are we using AI to deepen connections or to isolate? Are we building tools that serve humanity or tools that serve profit alone?

Intentional design is not just about avoiding harm; it is about actively creating good. It is about using AI to amplify the best of what it means to be human—our creativity, our compassion, and our capacity for growth.

The Future We Want to Build

The machines we build will shape the future, but they will not define it. That is up to us. As we stand at the threshold of an era defined by AI, we must ask ourselves what kind of world we want to create.

Do we want a future where technology deepens inequality or one where it promotes equity? Do we want a future where algorithms manipulate our attention or one where they enrich our understanding? Do we want a future where machines overshadow humanity or one where they enhance it?

These are not easy questions, and the answers will not be unanimous. But they are questions worth asking. Because the machines we build are not just tools—they are reflections of who we are and who we aspire to be.

A Mirror and a Challenge

Ultimately, the machines we build challenge us to confront ourselves. They reveal our priorities, our biases, and our blind spots. They force us to ask not only, "What can technology do?" but also, "What does it mean to be human?"

This challenge is both daunting and inspiring. It reminds us that the future is not something that happens to us—it is something we create. And in that creation, we have the opportunity to reflect not just what we are but what we can become.

Let us meet this challenge with courage, wisdom, and humanity. Let us build machines that reflect our highest ideals and that remind us, in their design and their use, of the infinite thread that connects us all.

Teaching Compassion to Machines

Can artificial intelligence understand empathy—or is it uniquely human?

Empathy is the ability to feel what another person feels—to step into their shoes and view the world from their perspective. It is one of humanity's most profound capabilities, shaping relationships, fostering cooperation, and driving acts of kindness. But empathy is also a deeply personal experience, rooted in the emotional complexity of the human condition.

Can a machine, built on binary code and mathematical algorithms, ever truly understand what it means to empathize? Or are the depths of empathy bound to the unpredictability of human life—the memories, emotions, and experiences that no dataset can fully encapsulate?

Simulating Empathy vs. Feeling It

Artificial intelligence can simulate empathy, but that is not the same as feeling it. An AI system can analyze a user's tone of voice, choice of words, or physiological data to determine if they are upset, happy, or anxious. It can respond with preprogrammed phrases designed to comfort or support, even adapting its responses to suit the individual.

But is this empathy? A machine does not feel joy, sorrow, or compassion. It does not care, even if it acts as though it does. What it provides is a reflection of our understanding of empathy—a simulation constructed by humans who do feel and care.

This distinction matters. While simulated empathy can be useful—think of chatbots providing mental health support or customer service—it raises important ethical questions. Should we allow machines to appear more empathetic than they are? Is it misleading to give the illusion of compassion where none exists?

The Limits of Algorithms

Empathy is not just about recognizing someone else's emotions; it is about responding in a way that resonates with their unique experience. This requires nuance, intuition, and a deep understanding of context—qualities that machines struggle to replicate.

Algorithms excel at identifying patterns and predicting outcomes, but they lack the lived experience that gives human empathy its depth. They do not know what it feels like to lose a loved one, to face rejection, or to experience joy so overwhelming it brings tears. Without this understanding, AI can only approximate empathy, and even the most advanced systems risk falling short in moments that require genuine human connection.

The Role of AI in Supporting Empathy

While AI may never feel empathy, it can still play a role in fostering it. Consider how AI can analyze vast amounts of data to identify systemic inequalities or highlight stories of people whose voices are often unheard. By surfacing these insights, AI can help us better understand the struggles and perspectives of others, enabling us to act with greater compassion.

AI can also assist in bridging communication gaps. Language translation tools, for example, can help people connect across linguistic and cultural divides, facilitating empathy where it might otherwise falter. Similarly, AI-powered accessibility tools can empower individuals with disabilities, making the world more inclusive and compassionate.

In these ways, AI can amplify human empathy, not by replacing it but by supporting it.

The Dangers of Misplaced Trust

The risk of teaching machines to mimic empathy is that we may begin to place too much trust in them. As AI becomes more sophisticated, it may be tempting to turn to machines for emotional support, bypassing the vulnerabilities and complexities of human relationships.

But a machine cannot hold your hand when you're grieving, nor can it share the unspoken connection of a knowing glance. The danger is not just that we might rely on machines to provide emotional support, but that in doing so, we could lose touch with the messy, imperfect humanity that gives life its meaning.

Empathy is not just about understanding—it is about connection. And connection requires more than data; it requires presence, vulnerability, and the courage to truly see one another.

Can Machines Ever Truly Care?

The question of whether AI can truly care is as much philosophical as it is technical. Care implies intention, a desire to act in the best interest of another. AI, no matter how advanced, does not have desires. It does not choose to care; it is programmed to act as though it does.

This does not mean AI is without value. A machine that can simulate care may still provide comfort, much like a soft blanket or a favorite song. But it is important to recognize the limits of this comfort. Machines can enhance our lives, but they cannot replace the fundamental need for human connection.

A Vision for the Future

As we continue to develop AI, we must ask ourselves what role we want it to play in our emotional lives. Should it be a tool to support and enhance human empathy, or should it attempt to replicate it?

I believe the greatest potential of AI lies not in replacing human empathy but in augmenting it. By helping us see and understand each other more clearly, AI can act as a bridge, connecting people in ways that were once unimaginable.

But to achieve this, we must remain vigilant. We must design AI systems with transparency, accountability, and humility, always remembering that their purpose is to serve humanity, not to supplant it.

The Uniqueness of Empathy

In the end, empathy may remain uniquely human—and that is a good thing. It is our ability to feel deeply, to connect authentically, and to care unconditionally that defines us. AI can reflect and amplify these qualities, but it cannot originate them.

The machines we build will never understand what it means to be human, but they can remind us of what it means to be human. And in a world increasingly driven by technology, that may be their most important role.

The Code of Ethics

A roadmap for aligning technological progress with our deepest values

Technology is a double-edged sword. It has the power to heal or harm, to connect or isolate, to build or destroy. The question is not whether we will continue to innovate, but whether those innovations will reflect the values we hold most dear.

In the development of artificial intelligence, robotics, and other advanced technologies, we find ourselves at a crossroads. On one path lies progress unchecked—progress that prioritizes profit, speed, and efficiency at the expense of humanity. On the other lies a future where technological advancement is guided by principles that honor the dignity, diversity, and well-being of all people.

This chapter is about the latter path. It is about creating a code of ethics—a moral compass to ensure that the machines we build serve the best of what it means to be human.

Principle 1: Transparency

Technology thrives on complexity, but ethics

demands clarity. For AI systems to earn trust, they must be transparent about how they work, what data they use, and what decisions they make.

This means designing systems that can explain their processes in terms humans can understand. It means holding companies accountable for the algorithms they deploy. And it means empowering users to ask questions and demand answers. Transparency is not just a technical challenge; it is a moral obligation.

Principle 2: Equity

Innovation should benefit everyone, not just the privileged few. Yet, history has shown that technological progress often exacerbates existing inequalities.

A code of ethics for technology must prioritize equity, ensuring that the benefits of AI and automation are distributed fairly. This includes addressing biases in algorithms, creating access for underserved communities, and designing systems that actively combat, rather than perpetuate, discrimination.

Equity is not an afterthought—it must be embedded into the design and deployment of every technology we create.

Principle 3: Accountability

With great power comes great responsibility. When

a machine makes a mistake, who is held accountable? When an algorithm causes harm, who takes responsibility?

Accountability in technology means establishing clear lines of ownership and responsibility. It means ensuring that developers, companies, and governments are answerable for the consequences of their creations. And it means building systems with fail-safes, checks, and balances to prevent abuse and mitigate harm.

Without accountability, progress risks becoming reckless.

Principle 4: Privacy

In a world where data is currency, privacy is often the price we pay for convenience. But privacy is not a luxury—it is a fundamental human right.

A code of ethics for technology must safeguard this right, placing limits on data collection, storage, and use. It must give individuals control over their information and ensure that consent is meaningful, not buried in fine print.

Privacy is the foundation of trust. Without it, even the most advanced technologies will falter.

Principle 5: Sustainability

Technological progress cannot come at the expense

of the planet. The resources we consume, the energy we use, and the waste we produce all have consequences that extend far beyond the immediate benefits of innovation.

A sustainable approach to technology means designing systems that are energy-efficient, environmentally friendly, and mindful of their long-term impact. It means recognizing that the health of humanity is inseparable from the health of the Earth.

Principle 6: Human-Centered Design

At its core, technology is about people. It exists to solve human problems, enhance human lives, and expand human possibilities.

A code of ethics must prioritize human-centered design, ensuring that technology serves humanity rather than the other way around. This means creating systems that are intuitive, accessible, and respectful of human values. It means prioritizing empathy over efficiency and connection over control.

Human-centered design is not just good practice—it is a moral imperative.

Navigating the Gray Areas

Ethics is rarely black and white. The development of technology often involves trade-offs, compromises, and difficult choices. A code of ethics is not a rigid set of rules—it is a framework for navigating these gray areas with integrity.

For example, how do we balance the benefits of data-driven insights with the risks of surveillance? How do we encourage innovation while protecting against unintended harm? These are not easy questions, but they are essential ones.

By grounding our decisions in principles like transparency, equity, and accountability, we can navigate the complexities of technological progress with greater clarity and purpose.

A Shared Responsibility

Creating an ethical future is not the responsibility of developers or policymakers alone—it is a collective effort. It requires collaboration between technologists, ethicists, governments, businesses, and individuals.

Each of us has a role to play. As developers, we must design with intention. As users, we must question and demand accountability. As a society, we must establish norms and regulations that reflect our shared values.

The Legacy of Our Creations

The machines we build will outlast us. The algorithms we design will shape the lives of future generations. This is both a humbling and a daunting realization.

The question we must ask ourselves is this: What legacy do we want to leave behind? Will our creations reflect the best of who we are, or will they amplify our worst instincts?

A code of ethics is not just a roadmap for building better machines—it is a vision for building a better world. By aligning technological progress with our deepest values, we can create a future that is not only innovative but also just, compassionate, and profoundly human.

Let us build with care. Let us build with courage. Let us build with ethics.

The Edge of the Singularity

What happens when machines think faster than we ever could?

Approaching the Horizon

The concept of the singularity—the point at which artificial intelligence surpasses human intelligence—has long been a topic of fascination and debate. It is a horizon both feared and revered, a moment that promises to redefine our understanding of life, work, and purpose.

But what happens when machines think faster, learn faster, and adapt faster than we ever could? Will they become our partners in solving the world's most complex problems? Or will their capabilities outpace our ability to control them, creating unforeseen risks and challenges?

These questions are no longer theoretical. As AI systems grow more advanced, the singularity moves from the realm of science fiction to a future we must prepare for.

The Speed of Thought

Human thought is remarkable but limited by biology. Neural signals travel at approximately 120 meters per second, a speed dwarfed by the near-instantaneous processing capabilities of modern machines. As AI systems evolve, their ability to process information, simulate outcomes, and adapt strategies will surpass anything the human brain can achieve.

This speed offers extraordinary potential. Imagine AI systems capable of designing vaccines in hours, solving environmental crises in days, or unraveling the mysteries of the universe in weeks. The acceleration of thought could propel humanity into an era of unprecedented discovery.

But this same speed poses risks. Decisions made in milliseconds may outstrip our ability to evaluate their implications. The faster machines think, the harder it becomes to ensure their actions align with human values.

Beyond Human Comprehension

As machines surpass human intelligence, they may begin to operate in ways that are difficult—or impossible—for us to understand. Today, even the creators of advanced neural networks sometimes struggle to explain how their algorithms arrive at certain conclusions.

At the edge of the singularity, this "black box" problem becomes more profound. Machines could develop strategies, systems, or solutions that work perfectly but defy human logic. This raises an unsettling question: How do we trust something we cannot fully comprehend?

Trust, in this context, becomes a critical issue. If we cannot understand the mechanisms behind machine decisions, we must find new ways to evaluate their reliability and safety. Transparency, oversight, and rigorous testing will be essential, but they may not always be sufficient.

The Power Dynamic

The singularity also forces us to confront questions about power. If machines surpass human intelligence, who will control them? Will their capabilities be harnessed for the collective good, or will they serve the interests of a select few?

The concentration of power in the hands of those who control advanced AI could exacerbate inequalities, creating a world where decisions affecting billions are made by machines operating at the behest of a privileged elite.

Avoiding this outcome requires proactive governance, ethical frameworks, and global cooperation. The singularity is not just a technological milestone—it is a societal challenge that demands foresight and collaboration.

What It Means to Be Human

At its core, the singularity is not just about machines—it is about us. What does it mean to be human in a world where machines surpass our cognitive abilities? What value do we bring to a future defined by hyper-intelligent systems?

The answer lies not in competing with machines but in embracing what makes us unique. While AI excels at processing data and solving complex problems, it cannot replicate the depth of human emotion, the richness of creativity, or the moral intuition that guides our decisions.

As machines take over tasks that once defined human effort, we have an opportunity to redefine our purpose. This is not a loss—it is an evolution. Freed from the constraints of routine labor and decision-making, we can focus on what truly matters: connection, meaning, and the pursuit of wisdom.

The Ethical Imperative

The edge of the singularity is not a point of no return—it is a choice. The technologies we create will reflect the values we prioritize. If we approach this moment with humility, foresight, and ethical intent, the singularity can be a force for good.

This means embedding safeguards into AI systems, creating mechanisms for accountability, and ensuring that the benefits of advanced intelligence are shared equitably. It means prioritizing transparency, fairness, and inclusivity in every step of development.

Most importantly, it means recognizing that the singularity is not just a technical challenge—it is a moral one.

Facing the Unknown

The singularity represents a journey into uncharted territory. We cannot predict exactly what will happen when machines surpass human intelligence, but we can prepare. We can approach this moment with curiosity, caution, and a commitment to the values that define us.

As we stand on the edge of this horizon, let us remember that the singularity is not the end of humanity—it is a new beginning. It is an opportunity to expand our understanding of intelligence, to amplify our potential, and to create a future that honors the infinite thread connecting us all.

The edge of the singularity is not something to fear—it is something to face, together.

Part III: The Philosophy of Progress

The Meaning We Invent

In a universe indifferent to our existence, how do we create purpose?

A Silent Universe

The universe is vast, indifferent, and silent. Stars burn, galaxies collide, and black holes consume everything in their path without regard for the creatures who gaze at them in awe. For centuries, humanity has grappled with this silence, searching for meaning in a cosmos that offers no answers.

Yet, it is precisely this indifference that defines our challenge—and our opportunity. If the universe does not grant us meaning, we are free to create it. This act of invention, this defiance of the void, is one of humanity's greatest triumphs.

The Myths We Tell Ourselves

Throughout history, we have sought purpose in

myths, religions, and philosophies. These stories have given us frameworks for understanding our place in the cosmos, offering meaning where none was evident.

But the meaning we derive from these narratives is not imposed by the universe; it is born from within us. When we look to the stars and see gods, when we contemplate nature and see beauty, when we endure suffering and find hope, we are inventing meaning.

Far from being a limitation, this act of invention is a profound expression of our humanity. It allows us to transcend the indifference of the universe and to see ourselves as creators of purpose.

The Search for Individual Meaning

For many, the search for meaning is deeply personal. It is found not in grand cosmic truths but in the small, intimate moments that define our lives: the laughter of a friend, the touch of a loved one, the satisfaction of work well done.

These moments remind us that meaning does not have to be universal to be profound. The universe may not care, but we do. And in our caring, we create a sense of purpose that is uniquely ours.

In my own life, I have found meaning in the act of inquiry—asking questions, seeking answers, and sharing what I learn. I have also found it in connection, in the relationships that ground me and the moments of vulnerability that remind me of what it means to be human.

Collective Meaning

While meaning is often personal, it is also collective. Communities, cultures, and societies create shared narratives that bind us together and give our lives direction. These narratives take many forms: traditions, laws, art, and even the technologies we build.

Consider the moon landing. As a scientific achievement, it was extraordinary. But as a shared moment of human endeavor, it was transformative. It was not just about reaching the moon—it was about what that journey represented: curiosity, courage, and the belief that we can transcend our limitations.

Collective meaning is powerful because it connects us. It reminds us that we are part of something larger than ourselves, and that our actions ripple outward, affecting others in ways we may never fully understand.

The Freedom to Choose

The absence of inherent meaning can feel daunting, even nihilistic. But it is also liberating. In a universe without preordained purpose, we are free to define our own.

This freedom comes with responsibility. The choices we make, the values we uphold, and the goals we pursue shape not only our lives but also the world around us. In this way, creating meaning is not just an act of personal fulfillment—it is an ethical act, a way of contributing to the collective story of humanity.

The Role of Technology in Meaning

As we build machines that increasingly shape our lives, we must ask how they influence our search for meaning. Does technology connect us or isolate us? Does it enrich our lives or distract us from what matters?

The technologies we create are not neutral; they reflect our priorities and values. If we want them to enhance our sense of purpose, we must design them with intention. This means building systems that amplify our ability to connect, to create, and to grow—not systems that exploit our vulnerabilities or reduce us to data points.

Technology, like the universe, does not inherently care. But we can imbue it with meaning by aligning it with our deepest values.

Living with the Mystery

The search for meaning is not something we resolve once and for all. It is a continuous process, a journey that evolves as we grow and change.

There will always be questions we cannot answer, mysteries we cannot solve. But perhaps that is the point. The act of searching, of striving to understand, is itself a form of meaning. It is a way of affirming that, despite the indifference of the universe, our existence matters—if only to us.

A Universe of Possibilities

In the face of an indifferent universe, our greatest power is our ability to care. We care about the people we love, the ideas we pursue, and the world we inhabit. This caring is the foundation of the meaning we invent.

The universe does not give us meaning, but it gives us possibilities. It gives us the raw materials—atoms, energy, time—with which we can create lives of purpose and beauty.

It is up to us to decide how we will use them.

Let us choose to create meaning that uplifts, that connects, and that inspires. Let us choose to see the indifference of the universe not as a void to be feared but as a canvas on which we paint our lives. Let us choose to care, and in doing so, to create a story worth telling.

Free Will Is an Illusion, and That's Okay

Wrestling with determinism and finding freedom within it

The Puzzle of Free Will

Few questions have haunted human thought more persistently than the question of free will. Do we truly make choices, or are our actions determined by forces beyond our control? Neuroscience, physics, and philosophy each weigh in with their own perspectives, yet the debate remains unresolved.

Science offers compelling evidence that much of what we do is dictated by factors outside our conscious awareness. Neural activity in the brain often precedes our awareness of making a decision. The physical universe, governed by cause and effect, suggests that every action is the inevitable result of what came before it.

At first glance, this determinism seems to rob life of meaning. If our choices are illusions, are we merely passengers on a preordained ride? But this perspective misses something vital: the illusion of choice is still profoundly real to us, and within that illusion lies a kind of freedom.

The Machinery of Choice

Consider the complexity of what we call a decision. Every choice we make is influenced by an intricate web of experiences, memories, genetics, and environmental factors. These influences shape our preferences, fears, and aspirations, often in ways we barely comprehend.

Yet, the experience of making a choice feels deeply personal. When we decide to forgive someone, take a new job, or pursue a dream, we feel agency. This feeling may be an emergent property of complex systems—our brains processing inputs and generating outputs—but that does not make it meaningless.

Our subjective experience of free will is a testament to the richness of human consciousness. Even if our choices are determined, the process of wrestling with them, weighing options, and reflecting on outcomes gives life its texture and depth.

Determinism as a Framework

Rather than seeing determinism as a threat to free will, we can view it as a framework that deepens our understanding of ourselves. Recognizing that our actions are shaped by causes allows us to approach life with greater humility and compassion.

If free will is an illusion, then so is the notion of complete self-sufficiency. None of us are truly "self-made." We are shaped by our environments, supported by others, and influenced by forces we cannot see. Understanding this can foster empathy, helping us see others not as isolated actors but as participants in a shared, interconnected system.

Freedom Within the Illusion

Even if free will is an illusion, it is a useful one. It allows us to take responsibility for our actions, to strive for growth, and to imagine new possibilities. The fact that our choices are influenced by prior causes does not negate their significance—it gives them context.

Imagine a river flowing toward the ocean. The river's path is determined by the contours of the land, the pull of gravity, and the volume of water it carries. Yet, within these constraints, the river moves dynamically, carving new channels, shaping landscapes, and finding its way.

We, too, flow within constraints. Our choices are shaped by biology, culture, and circumstance, but within these boundaries, we find room to act. We find freedom not in escaping causality but in navigating it with intention and awareness.

Reframing Responsibility

Determinism does not absolve us of responsibility—it redefines it. If our actions are influenced by external factors, then so are the actions of others.

This understanding can inspire systems of justice, education, and governance that emphasize rehabilitation over punishment, support over blame.

Responsibility, in this view, is not about absolute freedom but about doing our best with the tools and circumstances we've been given. It is about recognizing our power to influence others and using that power wisely.

The Role of Consciousness

One of the great mysteries of life is why we are conscious at all. If our actions are determined by cause and effect, why do we experience them as choices? Perhaps consciousness is not about controlling outcomes but about witnessing them.

In this sense, consciousness becomes a kind of participatory observation, allowing us to engage with the world in ways that enrich our understanding and experience. The illusion of free will may be consciousness's greatest gift, giving us a sense of agency and a platform for creativity, connection, and meaning.

Making Peace with the Illusion

Accepting that free will is an illusion does not diminish life's beauty—it enhances it. It reminds us that every moment is the result of countless interactions, stretching back through time in an unbroken chain. It shows us that our lives are not solitary but interwoven with the fabric of the universe.

Rather than resisting determinism, we can embrace it as a source of wonder. We can marvel at the intricate forces that shape us, from the neurons firing in our brains to the gravitational pull of distant stars. And within this vast, determined system, we can still find meaning in the choices we experience as our own.

The Freedom to Respond

While we may not control the circumstances of our lives, we do have the power to respond to them. Viktor Frankl, a Holocaust survivor, wrote that between stimulus and response lies a space. In that space lies our freedom.

This freedom is not about breaking free from causality—it is about choosing how we engage with it. It is about finding purpose in the face of adversity, love in the face of loss, and growth in the face of challenge.

A Universe of Possibilities

If free will is an illusion, it is a beautiful one—a testament to the complexity of life and the depth of human experience. It allows us to navigate a determined world with curiosity, compassion, and creativity.

We may not control the flow of the river, but we can shape its course. We can carve meaning from the landscape of existence, finding freedom not in escaping the universe's laws but in living fully within them.

And that, perhaps, is the greatest act of free will: embracing the illusion and making it our own.

Time is an Illusion, Too

Exploring the nature of time, memory, and our fleeting moments of awareness

The Paradox of Time

Time feels like the most tangible aspect of our lives—an unyielding force that governs everything we do. We measure it, race against it, and long for more of it. Yet, at its core, time is not what it seems.

Physicists tell us that time is not an absolute; it is a dimension intertwined with space, shaped by gravity and motion. To an observer traveling at the speed of light, time as we know it would cease to exist. Philosophers argue that the present moment is a fleeting construct, caught between a past we cannot change and a future we cannot know.

If time is an illusion, what does that mean for the way we live? How do we reconcile our perception of time with its elusive, almost fictional nature?

The Subjective Experience of Time

Time is not a uniform experience. An hour spent waiting feels longer than an hour spent laughing with friends. A day in childhood feels infinite, while decades in adulthood seem to vanish in the blink of an eye.

This subjectivity reveals something profound: time is not just a measure of external events; it is deeply tied to our awareness, emotions, and memory. When we are fully present, time slows down, stretching to accommodate the richness of our experience. When we are distracted or disengaged, time accelerates, slipping through our fingers like sand.

The illusion of time is not just a matter of physics—it is a reflection of how we live and what we value.

Memory and the Fabric of Time

Our understanding of time is inextricably linked to memory. The past exists only as a series of recollections, shaped and reshaped by our minds. We do not remember moments as they were; we remember them as we perceived them, filtered through the lens of emotion, context, and hindsight.

In this way, memory is both a gift and a limitation. It allows us to carry the essence of our experiences forward, connecting who we were with who we are. But it also distorts, blurs, and omits, creating a narrative of time that is uniquely personal and fundamentally imperfect.

The future, too, exists only in our imagination. It is a projection, a canvas onto which we paint our hopes, fears, and ambitions. In reality, the only time that truly exists is now—a fleeting moment that vanishes as soon as we try to grasp it.

The Present as a Portal

If the past is memory and the future is imagination, the present is where life happens. Yet, it is also the most elusive of the three. We spend much of our lives caught in a tug-of-war between regret for what was and anxiety about what will be, neglecting the moment unfolding before us.

This is one of the great challenges of being human: to live fully in the present while honoring the past and preparing for the future. It requires a kind of mindfulness—a willingness to be awake to the texture of now, to savor its fleeting beauty without clinging to it.

The present is not static; it is a portal, a point of infinite potential where the stories of our lives are written one decision at a time.

The Illusion of Control

Time often feels like something we must manage, an enemy to outwit or a resource to conserve. But this mindset creates a paradox: the more we try to control time, the less we feel in control.

We pack our schedules, race against deadlines, and measure productivity in hours and minutes, only to find ourselves exhausted and unfulfilled. This illusion of control blinds us to the truth: time is not something we own; it is something we inhabit.

To live well is not to conquer time but to flow with it, to find harmony in its rhythms and gratitude in its passing.

Eternity in a Moment

There are moments that seem to transcend time—a sunset that takes your breath away, a conversation that lingers in your soul, a song that feels infinite in its beauty. These experiences remind us that time is not just a sequence of events; it is a vessel for meaning.

When we are fully present, time dissolves. A second can feel like an eternity, and an eternity can feel like a second. These moments of timelessness are not interruptions to life; they are life at its most profound.

Time, Technology, and Progress

In an age of instant communication and relentless acceleration, our relationship with time is more strained than ever. Technology promises to save us time, yet it often makes us feel like we have less of it.

AI and automation hold the potential to transform how we use time, freeing us from routine tasks and expanding our capacity for creativity and connection. But this potential can only be realized if we resist the urge to fill every freed moment with more busyness.

The true gift of technology is not efficiency but presence—the ability to focus on what matters most, unburdened by distractions.

Living Beyond the Illusion

To say that time is an illusion is not to dismiss its importance—it is to recognize its complexity. Time is both real and imagined, a framework that shapes our lives even as it eludes our grasp.

What matters is not how much time we have but how we spend it. Are we present for the moments that matter? Do we use our time to connect, to create, to grow?

The illusion of time is a reminder that life is fleeting, precious, and profoundly beautiful. By embracing this truth, we can live not in fear of time's passage but in awe of its possibilities.

The Gift of Awareness

In the end, time is not something to be conquered or understood—it is something to be experienced. It is the medium through which we live our lives, the thread that weaves together memory, imagination, and presence.

If we can learn to see time not as a constraint but as a gift, we will find freedom within its flow. We will discover that the moments we have, however fleeting, are enough.

And in those moments, we will glimpse eternity.

The Weight of Infinite Choices

Why our abundance of options paralyzes us—and how to overcome it

The Paradox of Choice

Modern life offers an abundance of choices. From the food we eat to the careers we pursue, from the books we read to the paths we take in relationships, we are surrounded by seemingly infinite options. At first glance, this abundance appears to be a gift—a testament to progress and freedom.

Yet, more often than not, it feels like a burden. The more options we have, the harder it becomes to choose. We second-guess our decisions, fear making the wrong choice, and sometimes avoid choosing altogether. This is the paradox of choice: abundance creates anxiety, not satisfaction.

The weight of infinite choices is not just a modern phenomenon; it is a deeply human struggle. But in a world of expanding possibilities, it is a challenge we must learn to navigate.

The Fear of Missing Out

One of the most insidious consequences of infinite choices is the fear of missing out. Every decision we make feels like a rejection of countless alternatives. When we choose one career, we close the door on others. When we commit to one person, we forgo the possibility of other connections.

This fear is amplified by a culture that idolizes potential and perfection. Social media feeds us curated images of other people's lives, making it easy to believe that better opportunities are always just out of reach. The result is a kind of paralysis, where the act of choosing becomes an act of loss.

But the truth is, no choice is perfect, and no path is without sacrifice. The fear of missing out is an illusion, rooted in the mistaken belief that there is a "right" choice waiting to be discovered.

The Tyranny of Optimization

The abundance of options also feeds into our obsession with optimization. We are constantly told to maximize our time, our resources, and our potential. This mindset turns every decision into a calculation, as though life were a series of equations to be solved.

But optimization comes at a cost. It reduces life's richness to a set of metrics, stripping away the spontaneity, uncertainty, and imperfection that make existence meaningful. When we focus too much on finding the "best" choice, we lose sight of the value in simply choosing.

Life is not a problem to be solved; it is an experience to be lived.

The Role of Intuition

In the face of infinite choices, intuition is often our greatest ally. While logic and analysis have their place, some decisions are too complex to be reduced to pros and cons. In these moments, it is intuition—our internal compass—that guides us.

Intuition is not irrational; it is the product of our experiences, values, and subconscious understanding. It is the quiet voice that tells us what feels right, even when the path ahead is unclear.

Learning to trust our intuition is not about ignoring logic; it is about balancing it with a deeper sense of what truly matters.

The Power of Commitment

One of the most liberating ways to overcome the weight of infinite choices is to embrace commitment. Choosing something—whether it's a career, a relationship, or a passion—does not limit our freedom; it gives it focus.

Commitment allows us to go deeper, to invest fully in the paths we choose. It frees us from the endless loop of "what if" and allows us to create meaning through action.

In my own life, I've found that some of the most fulfilling experiences come not from having infinite options but from fully embracing the ones I've chosen. Commitment is not a surrender; it is a declaration of purpose.

Finding Meaning in Imperfection

No choice is without flaws, and no path is without obstacles. The pursuit of perfection is a trap that leaves us perpetually dissatisfied. Instead of seeking the perfect choice, we can find meaning in the imperfect ones we make.

Every decision, no matter how small, is an opportunity to learn, grow, and connect. The act of choosing is not about finding the "right" answer—it is about engaging with life, embracing uncertainty, and discovering what matters most to us.

The Freedom of Letting Go

Sometimes, the weight of infinite choices comes from a belief that we must control every aspect of our lives. But true freedom lies not in controlling everything but in letting go of what we cannot control.

When we let go of the need to choose perfectly, we open ourselves to the beauty of serendipity. We allow ourselves to be surprised, to discover joy in the unexpected, and to find meaning in the choices we never planned to make.

A Path Forward

The abundance of options is not something to fear—it is something to navigate. By trusting our intuition, embracing commitment, and finding meaning in imperfection, we can lighten the weight of infinite choices.

Life's richness lies not in its abundance but in our engagement with it. The choices we make are not just decisions; they are acts of creation, shaping the stories of our lives.

In the end, the weight of infinite choices is a reminder of our freedom—the freedom to choose, to change, and to create meaning. Let us embrace that freedom with courage, gratitude, and an open heart.

Part IV: A Love Letter to Humanity

Why We Fight

The beauty in struggle and the grace in perseverance

The Inescapable Struggle

Life is struggle. From the moment we take our first breath, we are confronted by challenges—big and small, internal and external. We struggle to survive, to connect, to find meaning, and to leave a mark on the world.

But struggle is not merely an obstacle; it is an essential part of what makes us human. It shapes us, teaches us, and calls forth our greatest strengths. Without struggle, there can be no growth, no transformation, and no triumph.

To fight—to strive against adversity—is not a sign of weakness but of vitality. It is a declaration that life, for all its difficulties, is worth the effort.

The Dual Nature of Struggle

Struggle has a dual nature: it is both painful and beautiful. The pain is undeniable, whether it comes from loss, failure, or fear. Yet, within that pain lies the seed of something extraordinary. It is through struggle that we discover who we are and what we are capable of.

Consider the athlete pushing through exhaustion, the artist wrestling with self-doubt, or the parent sacrificing for their child. In each case, the struggle is not separate from the beauty of the endeavor—it is the very source of it.

Struggle reminds us that life's most meaningful moments are not handed to us; they are earned.

The Grace in Perseverance

Perseverance is not about ignoring pain or pretending that struggle doesn't exist. It is about moving forward in spite of it. It is about finding the courage to continue when the path is unclear and the destination feels out of reach.

In my own life, I have often found grace in the act of persevering. Whether it's wrestling with a difficult problem in AI research or navigating personal challenges, the decision to keep going has always brought unexpected insights and rewards.

Perseverance is not about never falling—it is about rising after every fall. It is about trusting that the effort itself has value, even if the outcome remains uncertain.

The Stories We Carry

Every human life is a story, and every story is filled with struggle. These stories connect us, reminding us that we are not alone in our fight.

When we share our struggles—openly and honestly—we create space for empathy and understanding. We see ourselves in others, and they see themselves in us. This shared humanity is a source of strength, reminding us that our individual battles are part of a larger, collective journey.

Some of the most inspiring stories I've encountered are not about people who avoided struggle but about those who faced it with courage and grace. They remind us that struggle is not something to be ashamed of—it is something to honor.

The Fight for Meaning

At its core, our struggle is a fight for meaning. We fight to build lives that matter, to create connections that endure, and to leave the world better than we found it.

This fight is not always dramatic; often, it is found in the quiet, everyday choices we make: to show kindness when it's easier to turn away, to pursue a dream despite setbacks, to stand up for what we believe in.

Meaning is not something we discover—it is something we fight for, moment by moment, decision by decision.

The Role of Struggle in Progress

Struggle is not just personal; it is also collective. Every leap forward in human history—from the abolition of slavery to the fight for civil rights to the exploration of space—has been born of struggle.

Progress is never easy. It requires effort, sacrifice, and perseverance. But it is through struggle that we build a better future, not just for ourselves but for generations to come.

When we fight for justice, equality, and understanding, we honor the struggles of those who came before us and lay the groundwork for those who will follow.

The Beauty of the Fight

There is beauty in the fight—not because it is easy but because it is meaningful. To fight is to care, to hope, and to believe in something greater than ourselves. It is to affirm that life, for all its challenges, is worth the effort.

The beauty of the fight lies in its ability to transform us. It pushes us to grow, to connect, and to discover depths of resilience and courage we didn't know we had.

Grace in Letting Go

Not every fight is meant to be won. Sometimes, grace is found not in persevering but in letting go—in accepting what cannot be changed and finding peace within it.

This, too, is a kind of struggle: the struggle to surrender, to forgive, and to embrace the impermanence of life. But even in these moments, there is beauty and strength.

Why We Fight

We fight because we care. We fight because we love. We fight because, in the face of adversity, we refuse to give up on ourselves, each other, or the world.

To fight is to live. It is to engage fully with the complexity of existence, to find meaning in the struggle, and to create beauty from chaos.

This is why we fight—not to avoid struggle but to embrace it, to transform it, and to use it as a force for good.

In our struggles, we find our humanity. And in our humanity, we find the infinite thread that connects us all.

The Fragility of Peace

Lessons from history, science, and human nature on why harmony is worth striving for

The Elusive Nature of Peace

Peace, in its simplest definition, is the absence of conflict. Yet, in practice, peace is far more complex and fragile. It is not merely the silencing of guns or the signing of treaties; it is the delicate balance of understanding, trust, and cooperation.

History reminds us of how fleeting peace can be. Empires rise and fall, wars ignite over resources, ideologies clash, and human ambition often destabilizes hard-won harmony. Despite our best efforts, peace remains one of humanity's most challenging pursuits—and one of its most vital.

The Biological Roots of Conflict

Human nature is, in part, shaped by competition. Our ancestors fought for survival in a world of scarce resources, and this evolutionary history is written into our DNA. We are wired to protect our own, to seek advantage, and to respond to perceived threats with aggression.

Yet, alongside this instinct for conflict, there exists a parallel drive for connection. Cooperation has been just as essential to our survival as competition. Our ability to work together, to form communities, and to empathize with others is what has allowed us to build civilizations, create art, and explore the cosmos.

Peace, then, is not the absence of struggle but the triumph of our cooperative instincts over our divisive ones. It is a choice—a fragile, deliberate choice—that must be made again and again.

The Lessons of History

History offers countless examples of peace achieved and peace lost. The Treaty of Versailles, meant to bring an end to World War I, sowed the seeds of resentment that led to World War II. The Cold War, marked by a precarious balance of power, demonstrated how close humanity can come to self-destruction.

Yet, history also provides hope. The formation of the United Nations, the civil rights movement, and the fall of apartheid in South Africa show that peace is possible when people come together with courage and vision.

These examples teach us that peace is not a passive state—it is an active process. It requires vigilance, compromise, and a willingness to confront the underlying causes of conflict.

The Science of Harmony

Scientific research provides valuable insights into how peace can be sustained. Studies on negotiation show the importance of empathy and understanding, while experiments in behavioral economics reveal how trust can be built through small, consistent acts of reciprocity.

Neuroscience, too, sheds light on the mechanisms of conflict and cooperation. Our brains are deeply attuned to social signals, capable of detecting both threats and opportunities for connection. By fostering environments that emphasize shared goals and mutual respect, we can activate the neural pathways that promote collaboration rather than division.

Technology can play a role as well. From communication platforms that bridge cultural divides to data-driven tools that predict and prevent conflict, science offers powerful tools for building a more peaceful world. But these tools must be wielded with care, guided by ethical principles and a commitment to humanity.

The Fragility of Trust

At the heart of peace lies trust, and trust is inherently fragile. It takes time to build and moments to destroy. One broken promise, one act of betrayal, can undo years of progress.

This fragility makes peace both precious and

precarious. It requires constant nurturing, through dialogue, transparency, and accountability. It requires humility—the recognition that no one has all the answers—and courage to seek common ground even when it feels out of reach.

The Cost of Peace

Peace is not free. It demands sacrifices—of ego, of pride, and sometimes of justice. Compromise often means accepting less than we believe we deserve, and reconciliation often requires forgiveness that feels undeserved.

Yet, the cost of peace is always less than the cost of war. Conflict tears apart families, destroys communities, and leaves scars that last for generations. The effort required to maintain peace pales in comparison to the devastation wrought by its absence.

The Beauty of Harmony

When peace is achieved, its beauty is undeniable. It is found in the laughter of children who grow up without fear, in the creativity that flourishes when people feel secure, and in the connections that deepen when trust is strong.

Peace allows us to dream, to build, and to thrive. It creates the conditions for human potential to be realized, enabling us to focus not on survival but on progress.

A Call to Action

Peace is fragile, but it is not impossible. It begins with small acts: a conversation that bridges a divide, a gesture of kindness that defuses tension, a decision to listen rather than retaliate.

On a larger scale, peace requires leadership, vision, and collective effort. It demands that we prioritize understanding over dominance, equity over exploitation, and compassion over indifference.

The pursuit of peace is not the absence of struggle but the willingness to struggle for a better world. It is a choice we must make not just once but every day, in every interaction, and in every decision.

Why Harmony Is Worth Striving For

Peace is not just the absence of conflict—it is the presence of possibility. It is the foundation upon which we build families, communities, and civilizations. It is the space in which we explore, create, and connect.

In a world as interconnected and interdependent as ours, peace is not a luxury—it is a necessity. It is the only path that allows us to face the challenges of the future together, as one humanity united by a shared destiny.

Let us strive for peace not because it is easy but because it is worth it. Let us honor its fragility by protecting it with vigilance and nurturing it with love. And let us remember that, in the words of Martin Luther King Jr., "Peace is not merely a distant goal that we seek, but a means by which we arrive at that goal."

Peace is our greatest challenge and our greatest hope. Let us rise to meet it.

To the Child I Was, and the Child I Will Never Meet

A meditation on legacy and the responsibility we owe to future generations

There is a photograph of me as a child, clutching a toy spaceship, staring out at a world I had barely begun to understand. In that moment, I am filled with wonder, curiosity, and the boundless optimism that only children possess. I did not yet know the weight of responsibility or the complexities of the world. All I knew was that the stars seemed impossibly far away, and I wanted to reach them.

Looking back, I realize that the child I was shaped the person I became. His curiosity fueled my desire to learn, his wonder became my love for science, and his dreams inspired me to keep striving, even when the path ahead seemed uncertain.

But I also realize how much I owe to him. His innocence and hope remind me why I do what I do. The questions he asked—the big, impossible ones about life, love, and the universe—still guide me today. They remind me that our greatest aspirations often come from the simplest places: a desire to understand, to connect, and to make the world a little better.

To the Child I Will Never Meet

There is another child I think about sometimes—the child I will never meet. This child exists in the future, shaped by choices I will never see, living in a world I will never know. Yet, this child is connected to me, just as I am connected to those who came before.

To this child, I owe a legacy. I owe the promise that the world I leave behind will be one worth inheriting. This is not a responsibility I take lightly. The choices we make today—in science, in technology, in how we treat one another—will ripple across time, shaping the lives of those who come after us.

I think about the technologies we build, the values we instill, and the systems we create. Will they empower this child, or will they burden them? Will they amplify their humanity, or will they diminish it? These questions guide me, reminding me that progress is not just about what we achieve but about what we preserve.

The Fragility of Legacy

Legacy is a fragile thing. It is not the monuments we build or the accolades we earn—it is the impact we leave on others, the values we pass down, and the ways we make the world better, even in small, unnoticed ways.

When I think about legacy, I think about the quiet acts of care and courage that ripple through time. The teacher who inspires a student. The parent who sacrifices for their child. The scientist who works tirelessly to solve a problem they may never see resolved.

These are the legacies that endure—not because they are grand, but because they are rooted in love, in humanity, and in the belief that the future matters.

The Responsibility We Carry

As individuals, we cannot control the course of history, but we can shape the threads of it. Each decision we make—what we create, how we treat others, the values we choose to uphold—contributes to the tapestry of the future.

This responsibility is both humbling and empowering. It reminds us that we are not just living for ourselves; we are part of a continuum, connected to the past and the future. The actions we take today will echo in the lives of those who follow.

This is not a burden—it is a gift. It gives our lives meaning and purpose, grounding our choices in something larger than ourselves.

A Letter Across Time

If I could write a letter to the child I will never meet, it might go something like this:

Dear Child,

I don't know what your world looks like. I don't know what challenges you face or what dreams you hold. But I want you to know this: we tried.

We tried to build a world that honors your potential, that cherishes your humanity, and that leaves space for you to dream your own dreams. We didn't always succeed, and I'm sorry for the times we fell short. But we never stopped believing in the future—in you.

You are the culmination of choices made by people who will never know you, but who cared about you all the same. Carry that knowledge with you, and let it inspire you to care for those who come after you, just as we cared for you.

With hope,

A Stranger Who Believed in You

Living for the Future

Legacy is not about perfection—it is about intention. It is about striving to leave the world better than we found it, even if our efforts are incomplete.

To the child I was, I owe the courage to dream. To the child I will never meet, I owe the determination to act. And to all the children of the world—past, present, and future—I owe my humanity, my hope, and my love.

This is the infinite thread that connects us: the belief

that our lives, however fleeting, can contribute to something enduring. Let us honor that thread by living with purpose, creating with care, and loving with all that we have.

The Simple Truths We Forget

What I've learned about living well, thinking deeply, and loving fully

The Power of Presence

In a world that moves at the speed of data, it's easy to lose ourselves in the endless stream of notifications, goals, and distractions. Yet, the most profound moments of life often happen when we slow down, when we pause long enough to be truly present.

Living well begins with presence. It's in the laughter of a friend, the stillness of a sunrise, the warmth of a hand held tightly in yours. These are the moments that ground us, that remind us life is not a checklist to complete but a series of fleeting miracles to be experienced.

Presence is simple, but not easy. It requires intention—the courage to step away from the noise and into the fullness of now.

The Courage to Wonder

One of the simplest yet most transformative truths

I've learned is this: curiosity is the antidote to stagnation. To think deeply is to ask questions—not just of the world, but of ourselves.

Why are we here? What does it mean to live a good life? How can we grow, love, and create in ways that matter? These questions have no definitive answers, but the act of asking them shapes us. It opens our minds, sharpens our perspectives, and fuels our pursuit of meaning.

Wonder is not a luxury; it is a necessity. It keeps us humble in the face of the unknown and inspires us to keep searching, even when the answers elude us.

The Grace of Imperfection

We live in a world that glorifies perfection, yet life itself is beautifully imperfect. We make mistakes, encounter failures, and face challenges that leave us bruised and vulnerable.

But it is in these imperfections that we find our humanity. They teach us resilience, compassion, and humility. They remind us that growth is not a straight line but a messy, unpredictable journey.

Loving fully means embracing imperfection—not just in others, but in ourselves. It means showing up with our flaws and fears, trusting that we are worthy of connection, not despite our imperfections but because of them.

The Strength in Kindness

Kindness is often dismissed as softness, but in truth, it is one of the greatest strengths we possess. It takes courage to be kind in a world that can be harsh, to choose empathy when it's easier to look away.

Living well means recognizing that every interaction is an opportunity to leave someone's life a little brighter. A kind word, a small gesture, or even a simple acknowledgment can ripple outward in ways we may never see.

Kindness is not just an action; it is a way of being—a commitment to see the humanity in others and to honor it with love.

The Freedom of Letting Go

We hold tightly to so many things: grudges, expectations, fears. But in clinging to these, we limit ourselves.

One of the simplest truths I've discovered is that freedom lies in letting go. Letting go of the need to control, the desire to be right, the fear of what might happen.

This doesn't mean giving up—it means making space. Space for new experiences, new connections, and new possibilities. Letting go is not a loss; it is a liberation.

The Wisdom of Small Joys

Happiness is not a destination—it is a series of small, fleeting moments. The taste of a favorite meal, the sound of laughter, the quiet satisfaction of finishing a task well done.

Living well means paying attention to these small joys. It means finding gratitude in the ordinary, seeing beauty in the mundane. These moments are easy to overlook, but they are the threads that weave a life of meaning.

The Necessity of Love

At the heart of everything I've learned is this: love is the simplest and most profound truth. It is what connects us, sustains us, and gives life its deepest meaning.

Love takes many forms—romantic, platonic, familial, even love for the world itself. But at its core, love is the act of seeing and valuing another, of choosing connection over separation.

Loving fully means being vulnerable, taking risks, and opening ourselves to the possibility of heartbreak. It is not always easy, but it is always worth it.

Living the Simple Truths

The truths we forget are often the ones we need

most. Be present. Stay curious. Embrace imperfection. Be kind. Let go. Savor joy. Choose love.

These are not grand, complex ideas—they are simple, yet profound. They are the truths that make us human, that connect us to one another, and that guide us toward a life well lived.

In the end, the simplest truths are the hardest to master. But they are also the most rewarding. They remind us that life's beauty lies not in what we achieve but in how we live, think, and love.

Let us live these truths—not perfectly, but fully. Let us carry them forward, sharing them with others and passing them on to future generations. And let us never forget that, in the end, it is the simplest truths that hold the greatest wisdom.

Part V: The Infinite Thread

We Are the Universe Waking Up

What it means to be a conscious fragment of an unfathomable whole

A Universe That Knows Itself

The cosmos is vast, ancient, and incomprehensibly complex. Stars form and die, galaxies drift apart, and black holes devour light. For billions of years, this unfolding has continued, indifferent and silent. And yet, here we are—small, fragile, and aware.

In each of us, the universe has found a way to know itself. Our consciousness, our ability to question, reflect, and wonder, is not separate from the cosmos—it is an extension of it. We are not observers standing apart from the universe; we are participants, woven into its fabric.

To be human is to embody this awakening, to carry within us the spark of a cosmos that has, for reasons beyond comprehension, become self-aware.

The Fragility of Awareness

Consciousness is both miraculous and fragile. It is a rare phenomenon in a universe dominated by entropy, a fleeting light against an infinite darkness. Yet, its very rarity makes it precious.

Our awareness allows us to glimpse the infinite, to marvel at the beauty of a star-filled sky, and to ponder the mysteries of existence. It allows us to ask questions the universe itself cannot: Why are we here? What is our purpose? How should we live?

But awareness is also fleeting. Our lives are brief, our memories fragile, and our perspectives limited. This impermanence is not a flaw—it is a reminder to cherish the moments we have, to honor the gift of being awake in a universe that so often sleeps.

The Interconnected Whole

When we look deeply into the nature of existence, we see that nothing exists in isolation. The atoms in our bodies were forged in the hearts of stars. The air we breathe was exhaled by countless living beings before us. The thoughts we think are shaped by cultures, histories, and connections that span the globe.

We are not separate from the universe; we are intricately connected to it. Every action we take ripples outward, touching lives and landscapes we may never see. Every moment of awareness we experience is part of a larger, cosmic unfolding.

This interconnectedness is not just a fact of existence—it is a source of meaning. To recognize our place in the whole is to see that our lives, however small, are part of something infinitely larger.

The Responsibility of Awareness

With awareness comes responsibility. To be awake in the universe is to have the power to shape it—to create, to destroy, to connect, to divide. It is to carry the weight of knowing that our choices matter.

This responsibility is both daunting and inspiring. It challenges us to use our awareness not for selfish gain but for the greater good. It invites us to act with compassion, humility, and a sense of wonder, knowing that we are stewards of a precious and fragile moment in the cosmos.

The Mystery of Consciousness

For all our advancements in science and philosophy, consciousness remains a mystery. How does a collection of neurons and chemicals give rise to thought, feeling, and awareness? Why does the universe allow us to experience it, to question it, to find beauty in it?

These questions may never be fully answered, but perhaps that is their gift. Consciousness is not something to be solved; it is something to be experienced. It is the lens through which we encounter the infinite, the tool that allows us to seek meaning in a universe that offers none.

A Universe Waking Up

If we are the universe waking up, then our awareness is not just an individual phenomenon—it is a collective one. Each of us is a fragment of the whole, and together, we form a mosaic of consciousness that spans continents, cultures, and generations.

Our awakening is incomplete. There is still so much to learn, so much to explore, so much to understand. But in this incompleteness lies the beauty of our journey. To be awake is not to have all the answers—it is to live the questions, to embrace the unknown, and to find meaning in the search.

Honoring the Infinite Thread

The infinite thread that connects us is not a thing we can touch or measure—it is a truth we feel in our deepest moments of awareness. It is the realization that we are not alone, that we are part of a story that began long before us and will continue long after we are gone.

To honor this thread is to live with intention. It is to see the beauty in each moment, to act with love and care, and to remember that our lives, though brief, are profoundly significant.

The Gift of Being Awake

To be a conscious fragment of an unfathomable whole is both humbling and empowering. It reminds us that we are small, yet essential; fleeting, yet eternal; individuals, yet part of something infinite.

The universe has given us the gift of awareness. Let us use it to create, to connect, and to care. Let us wake up fully to the wonder of existence, embracing the infinite thread that binds us to each other and to the cosmos itself.

And let us never forget: we are the universe, awake and alive, marveling at its own beauty.

The Final Question

If life is a fleeting experiment in meaning, how do we live with courage and joy?

A Fleeting Experiment

Life is brief. In the cosmic scale, our existence is but a flicker, a momentary spark in an endless expanse of time and space. This fleeting nature can feel daunting, even overwhelming. But within it lies the very essence of life's beauty. The transience of existence doesn't diminish its value—it amplifies it.

To see life as an experiment in meaning is to embrace its uncertainty, its imperfection, and its impermanence. It is to recognize that we are not here to uncover a single truth but to explore the infinite possibilities of what it means to be alive.

The Courage to Embrace Uncertainty

Courage is not the absence of fear; it is the decision to move forward despite it. In a world where nothing is guaranteed and everything is transient, courage begins with acceptance.

We must accept that we will never have all the

answers, that loss is inevitable, and that the future is unknown. But this acceptance is not defeat—it is liberation. It frees us to act, to explore, and to create without waiting for certainty.

Living with courage means leaning into the unknown, trusting that the act of living itself is enough, even when the destination is unclear.

Finding Joy in the Experiment

Joy is not the absence of struggle; it is the presence of meaning. It is found not in the grand gestures or perfect moments but in the small, everyday experiences that connect us to life.

A shared laugh, a quiet sunset, the feeling of creating something that matters—these are the moments where joy resides. They remind us that meaning is not something we discover but something we cultivate, moment by moment.

To live with joy is to savor these moments, to find gratitude in the ordinary, and to approach life with a sense of play.

The Balance Between Striving and Surrender

Life is a paradox of effort and letting go. We strive to grow, to achieve, to create, yet we must also surrender to the forces we cannot control. This balance is not easy to find, but it is essential.

Striving without surrender leads to exhaustion and disillusionment. Surrender without striving leads to stagnation. The art of living lies in knowing when to push forward and when to let go, when to act and when to simply be.

Connection as a Source of Meaning

If life is fleeting, then our connections with others are among its most profound gifts. We find courage in the support of those who stand beside us, and we find joy in the love we share.

Connection reminds us that we are not alone, that our struggles and triumphs are part of a larger, shared story. Whether through relationships, community, or a sense of belonging to humanity itself, connection gives our lives depth and purpose.

The Legacy of Living Well

We may not have control over the length of our lives, but we do have control over their depth. To live well is to create a legacy not of monuments but of moments—a legacy of kindness, creativity, and love.

This legacy is not about being remembered but about the ripples we leave behind. Every act of care, every moment of presence, contributes to the infinite thread that connects us all.

The Courage to Ask and the Joy to Live

The final question—how to live with courage and joy—has no single answer. It is a question we answer daily, through the choices we make and the values we uphold.

To live with courage is to face the unknown with an open heart. To live with joy is to embrace the fleeting beauty of each moment. Together, they form the foundation of a meaningful life.

An Invitation to Live

If life is an experiment, let us approach it with curiosity and wonder. Let us take risks, make mistakes, and grow from them. Let us find meaning not in avoiding imperfection but in embracing it.

Let us live as though each moment matters, because it does. Let us connect, create, and care, knowing that our lives, however brief, are part of something infinite.

And let us ask, not with fear but with hope: If this is life's fleeting experiment in meaning, how will we live it?

The answer is ours to create, each day, each choice, and each moment. The infinite thread is waiting—let us weave it with courage and joy.

Love Is the Answer

A manifesto for humanity, rooted in the only constant that transcends time: love

The Universal Constant

In a universe defined by change—stars burning out, civilizations rising and falling, lives beginning and ending—love is the one constant that endures. It transcends time, space, and circumstance. It is the force that binds us to one another, the thread that weaves through every human story, connecting us across generations and distances.

Love is not just an emotion; it is a way of being. It is the decision to care, to act, and to create meaning in a world that often feels indifferent. It is the foundation of all that is good in humanity, and it is the answer to the questions that challenge us most deeply.

The Power of Love

Love is not weak or passive—it is the most powerful force we possess. It drives us to sacrifice for others, to persevere in the face of hardship, and to strive for a better world. It is what allows us to see beyond ourselves, to empathize, and to connect.

In a time when division and conflict often dominate, love is the antidote. It bridges divides, heals wounds, and inspires hope. It reminds us that, despite our differences, we are all part of the same human family.

A Choice We Make

Love is not something that simply happens to us—it is a choice we make, again and again. It is choosing to see the humanity in others, even when it's difficult. It is choosing compassion over judgment, understanding over indifference, and connection over isolation.

This choice is not always easy. Love asks us to be vulnerable, to forgive, and to let go of fear. But in making this choice, we unlock the greatest potential within ourselves and each other.

The Many Forms of Love

Love is not a single thing—it is infinite in its expressions. It is found in the quiet devotion of a parent, the unspoken bond between friends, the passion of a creative endeavor, and the awe we feel for the natural world.

Romantic love, familial love, platonic love, and even love for humanity itself—all are facets of the same fundamental force. Each form of love enriches our lives, reminding us that we are not alone, that we are seen, and that we matter.

Love as a Guiding Principle

If love is the answer, then it must guide not only our personal lives but also our collective actions. It must shape how we build societies, create technologies, and care for our planet.

A world built on love prioritizes equity over greed, understanding over power, and connection over division. It values people not for what they produce but for who they are. It sees progress not as an end in itself but as a means to deepen our shared humanity.

The Challenges of Love

Love is not easy. It requires courage, patience, and resilience. It asks us to confront our fears, to forgive when we've been hurt, and to persist when the world feels unkind.

Yet, it is precisely because love is challenging that it is so transformative. It pushes us to grow, to become more than we thought we could be, and to create a world that reflects our highest ideals.

The Legacy of Love

When we look back on our lives, it is not our achievements or possessions that will matter most—it is the love we gave and received. Love is the legacy we leave behind, the thread that connects us to those who came before and those who will follow.

It is in the small acts of kindness, the relationships we nurture, and the care we show for others that our true impact is felt.

A Manifesto for Humanity

If we are to thrive as individuals and as a species, love must be our guiding principle. It must inform how we treat one another, how we create, and how we live.

Let us build technologies that amplify connection, not division. Let us create societies that honor every person's dignity and worth. Let us care for our planet with the same love we show to those closest to us, knowing that it is our shared home.

Most importantly, let us remember that love is not just something we feel—it is something we do. It is an action, a choice, and a commitment to the infinite thread that binds us all.

The Answer We Already Know

The challenges we face are immense, but the answer has always been within us. Love is not a new idea—it is the oldest truth we know. It is the constant that transcends time, reminding us of who we are and who we can be.

In the end, love is the answer not because it solves every problem, but because it gives us the courage to face them. It is the thread that connects us, the light that guides us, and the force that makes life worth living.

Let us live with love, act with love, and build a future rooted in love. In doing so, we honor the infinite thread that connects us to one another and to the universe itself.

Love is the answer. It always has been. It always will be.

Epilogue

This Is Not the End

A closing reflection on why the greatest mysteries are the ones we never fully solve—and why that's exactly how it should be

The Unfinished Story

Life is an unfinished story. No matter how much we learn, create, or understand, there will always be more questions than answers, more possibilities than certainties. This is not a limitation; it is a gift.

The mysteries that remain unsolved are the ones that keep us moving forward. They inspire us to ask, to imagine, and to strive for more. They remind us that life is not about arriving at a destination but about exploring the infinite landscapes of what could be.

This is not the end because there is no end. There is only the ongoing journey—the infinite thread that connects us to each other, to the universe, and to the questions that define us.

The Beauty of the Unknown

There is a certain beauty in not knowing. The unanswered questions—What is consciousness? What is love? Why does the universe exist?—are not failures of understanding; they are invitations to wonder.

When we solve a mystery, it loses some of its magic. But the greatest mysteries are inexhaustible. They are like the stars in the night sky: no matter how many we map, their vastness remains.

To live well is not to conquer the unknown but to embrace it. It is to find joy in the search, to marvel at the complexity of existence, and to accept that some questions are too profound to be fully grasped.

A Thread That Continues

The infinite thread is not something we can unravel or complete—it is something we are part of, something we contribute to with every thought, action, and connection.

This thread does not belong to any one person, generation, or civilization. It is woven across time, linking us to those who came before and those who will come after. It is a reminder that, while our lives are brief, our impact is not.

Each of us adds our own color, texture, and meaning to this thread. And though our contributions may be small, they are essential to the larger tapestry of humanity.

Why the Journey Matters

If there is no end, then what gives life its meaning? The answer lies in the journey itself. The value of a question is not in the answer—it is in the asking. The purpose of a path is not to reach the destination but to walk it, to experience it, and to grow along the way.

The mysteries we cannot solve are not obstacles; they are companions. They walk with us, challenge us, and remind us that the universe is far greater than our understanding of it.

Living with the Unfinished

To live with the unfinished is to live with humility. It is to recognize that our knowledge, no matter how vast, will always be incomplete. But it is also to live with courage—the courage to face uncertainty, to ask questions that have no answers, and to find meaning in the search itself.

This is not resignation; it is liberation. It frees us from the need for certainty, allowing us to engage fully with the complexity and wonder of existence.

An Invitation to Continue

This book is not the end of the story. It is one thread in a larger, ongoing tapestry. The questions we have explored—about love, meaning, and the machines we build—are not meant to be resolved here. They are meant to inspire, to provoke, and to guide you on your own journey.

Take these questions with you. Add your own answers, your own insights, and your own mysteries. Share them with others, and let them weave their own threads into the fabric of humanity.

This Is Not the End

The greatest mysteries are the ones we never fully solve, because they are the ones that keep us alive. They give us purpose, connect us to each other, and remind us that we are part of something infinite.

This is not the end because the questions remain, the journey continues, and the thread goes on. And that is exactly how it should be.

Let us walk this path together, with curiosity, with courage, and with love. Let us celebrate the unfinished story of humanity, knowing that each of us is a vital part of the infinite thread.

And let us never stop asking, wondering, and creating—because in that, we find the essence of what it means to be alive.

Appendices

My most profound lessons from mentors, scientists, and thinkers

The Wisdom of Mentors

Throughout my life, I have been shaped by the wisdom of mentors—those who offered guidance not as answers but as questions, challenges, and examples of how to live fully and think deeply.

One mentor taught me the importance of humility in the face of complexity. "The moment you think you understand everything," he said, "is the moment you stop learning." This lesson has stayed with me, reminding me to approach every problem with curiosity and respect for its intricacies.

Another mentor emphasized the value of persistence. "Great work doesn't come from flashes of brilliance," they told me. "It comes from showing up, again and again, even when it's hard." This advice has been a beacon during moments of doubt, reminding me that perseverance is often the most powerful force we have.

Perhaps the most profound lesson I've learned from

mentors is this: the best teachers do not seek to be followed. They seek to inspire you to think for yourself, to question, and to grow.

Lessons from Scientists

The greatest scientists I've encountered share a common trait: a profound reverence for the unknown. They are not driven by the need for certainty but by a love for exploration.

From Albert Einstein, I learned the importance of simplicity. "Everything should be made as simple as possible," he said, "but no simpler." This principle has guided my work, encouraging me to distill complex ideas without oversimplifying them.

Richard Feynman's playful approach to learning taught me the joy of curiosity. "I'm not afraid of not knowing," he said. "I'm delighted by the questions." His perspective reminds me that science is not just a pursuit of answers—it is a celebration of wonder.

Carl Sagan's eloquence inspired me to see science as a bridge between knowledge and humanity. His ability to connect the cosmos to the human experience taught me that science is not just about understanding the universe—it is about finding our place within it.

Insights from Thinkers

Philosophy has been a constant companion in my

search for meaning. The thinkers who have most profoundly influenced me have challenged me to confront the deepest questions of existence.

From Søren Kierkegaard, I learned the courage it takes to embrace uncertainty. "Life can only be understood backwards," he wrote, "but it must be lived forwards." His words remind me that meaning is often found not in clarity but in the act of living itself.

Simone Weil's reflections on attention taught me the transformative power of focus. "Attention," she wrote, "is the rarest and purest form of generosity." This idea has shaped how I approach relationships, work, and even the smallest moments of daily life.

From Viktor Frankl, I learned that meaning is not something we find—it is something we create. His ability to find purpose even in the darkest circumstances taught me that meaning is always within our grasp, if we are willing to seek it.

The Common Threads

Across these lessons, I see common threads: humility, curiosity, persistence, and a deep respect for the unknown. These qualities are not just the foundation of great work—they are the foundation of a meaningful life.

Each of these mentors, scientists, and thinkers approached the world with a sense of wonder and responsibility. They understood that knowledge is not an end but a beginning, a tool to build connections, solve problems, and create a better future.

Carrying the Lessons Forward

These lessons are not static; they are alive, evolving with each new experience and challenge. They are not answers to be memorized but principles to be lived, questioned, and shared.

My hope is that, in sharing these lessons, they will inspire you to reflect on your own. Who has shaped your thinking? What insights have guided you? And how will you carry those lessons forward, weaving them into the infinite thread of humanity?

We are all students, and we are all teachers. The lessons we learn and the lessons we share are the legacy we leave behind. Let us honor that legacy by living with humility, curiosity, and love.

Annotated list of books, ideas, and moments that shaped this journey

Books That Opened My Eyes

1. **"Man's Search for Meaning" by Viktor Frankl**

    This book taught me that even in the darkest circumstances, the human spirit can find purpose. Frankl's insights into the interplay between suffering, meaning, and resilience profoundly shaped my understanding of what it means to live well.

2. **"The Structure of Scientific Revolutions" by Thomas Kuhn**

    Kuhn's exploration of paradigm shifts in science revealed the power of perspective. His ideas inspired me to see progress not as linear but as a series of transformative leaps, driven by curiosity and the willingness to challenge assumptions.

3. **"The Myth of Sisyphus" by Albert Camus**

    Camus's embrace of life's absurdity resonated deeply with me. His argument that we must imagine Sisyphus happy helped me see that meaning is something we create, not something we discover.

4. **"Cosmos" by Carl Sagan**

   Sagan's ability to connect the vastness of the universe with the intimacy of human experience reminded me that science and storytelling are deeply intertwined. His work continues to inspire me to explore and communicate with wonder.

5. **"Grit" by Angela Duckworth**

   This book reinforced the idea that persistence and passion outweigh innate talent. It gave me tools to think about perseverance not just as a personal quality but as a teachable, learnable practice.

Ideas That Transformed My Thinking

1. **The Trolley Problem (Ethics and AI)**

   This philosophical thought experiment shaped how I think about the moral dilemmas we face in designing AI systems. It challenges us to grapple with difficult trade-offs and reminds us that even simple decisions have complex ethical dimensions.

2. **The Observer Effect (Quantum Mechanics)**

   The idea that the act of observation can

influence outcomes has profound implications—not just in physics but in how we engage with the world. It reminds me that awareness and attention matter, both in science and in life.

3. **The Hero's Journey (Joseph Campbell)**

   Campbell's framework for storytelling revealed the universal patterns that connect human experiences. It showed me how deeply our narratives shape our sense of purpose and how technology itself is becoming part of these stories.

4. **The Hard Problem of Consciousness (Philosophy of Mind)**

   This idea continues to challenge and fascinate me. The question of how subjective experience arises from physical processes is one of the deepest mysteries of existence and a driving force behind my fascination with AI and the human condition.

Moments That Defined the Journey

1. **The First Time I Coded an Algorithm**

   I remember the sense of awe when I realized that a series of lines on a screen could model something real, something alive. It wasn't just about programming—it was about creating, exploring, and understanding the world in a new way.

2. **Sitting with My Grandfather Under the Stars**

   He didn't say much that night, but he didn't need to. The vastness of the sky and the quiet of his presence taught me that some of life's most profound lessons are unspoken.

3. **Failing Publicly**

   Presenting an idea that was torn apart during a conference was humiliating, but it was also a turning point. That failure taught me the importance of resilience and the value of criticism as a tool for growth.

4. **Holding Someone's Hand in the Final Moments**

   In that fragile space between life and death, I learned more about love and connection than I ever have in a book or classroom. It was a moment that stripped away everything unnecessary and revealed what truly matters.

5. **A Child Asking "Why?"**

   The simplicity of a child's endless "why?" reawakened my sense of wonder. It reminded me that every question, no matter how simple, holds the potential to unlock profound truths.

The Thread That Connects Them All

These books, ideas, and moments are more than just influences—they are pieces of the infinite thread that has shaped this journey. Each has left its mark, not as definitive answers but as invitations to think, feel, and grow.

If I've learned one thing from this collection of experiences, it's that the greatest lessons often come from unexpected places. They come from the ordinary, the extraordinary, and everything in between.

I share these with the hope that they will inspire you to reflect on your own journey, to seek out the books, ideas, and moments that resonate with you, and to weave them into the tapestry of your life.

The thread continues, and so does the search. Let us carry it forward together.

A short poem: *"To the Stars We Will Return."*

We are stardust, born of flame,

A fleeting spark with an ancient name.

Through time and space, we drift and yearn,

To the stars, we will return.

The cosmos whispers, vast and deep,

Of secrets held and truths that sleep.

Each moment's fleeting, yet we learn,

To the stars, we will return.

In love, in struggle, in dreams we find,

The threads that weave through humankind.

Though fragile hearts may ache and burn,

To the stars, we will return.

Not as we were, but as we've grown,

With knowledge shared and seeds we've sown.

The infinite calls, and so we turn—

To the stars, we will return.

This poem is both a reflection and a promise—a reminder of where we came from and where we are headed. It is a celebration of our journey, our curiosity, and the infinite thread that binds us to the universe and each other.